WRESTLING SUPERST★RS

REY MYSTERIO

BY BLAKE MARKEGARD

EPIC

BELLWETHER MEDIA • MINNEAPOLIS, MN

EPIC BOOKS are no ordinary books. They burst with intense action, high-speed heroics, and shadows of the unknown. Are you ready for an Epic adventure?

This edition first published in 2015 by Bellwether Media, Inc.

No part of this publication may be reproduced in whole or in part without written permission of the publisher. For information regarding permission, write to Bellwether Media, Inc., Attention: Permissions Department, 5357 Penn Avenue South, Minneapolis, MN 55419.

Library of Congress Cataloging-in-Publication Data

Markegard, Blake.
  Rey Mysterio / by Blake Markegard.
    pages cm. – (Epic: Wrestling Superstars)
  Includes bibliographical references and index.
  Summary: "Engaging images accompany information about Rey Mysterio. The combination of high-interest subject matter and light text is intended for students in grades 2 through 7"– Provided by publisher.
  ISBN 978-1-62617-143-5 (hardcover : alk. paper)
  1. Rey Mysterio–Juvenile literature. 2. Wrestlers–United States–Biography–Juvenile literature. I. Title.
  GV1196.R45M37 2014
  796.812092–dc23
  [B]
                        2014002071

Printed in the United States of America, North Mankato, MN.

TABLE OF CONTENTS

WARNING!

The wrestling moves used in this book are performed by professionals.
Do not attempt to reenact any of the moves performed in this book.

THE DEBUT

A masked man jumps inside the WWE ring. He is Rey Mysterio. He has acrobatic moves to try on Chavo Guerrero.

CHAVO GUERRERO

Guerrero is not intimidated. But Mysterio
surprises him with the 619. He swings
between the ropes for a takedown. Mysterio
is a "Flying Fury" in his debut!

WHO IS REY MYSTERIO?

Rey Mysterio is WWE's Mexican mystery. He hides his face with a mask like Mexico's luchadores. His name also means "King of Mystery" in Spanish.

Mysterio's mask is important to his character. WWE blurs Mysterio's face when he is unmasked.

LIFE BEFORE WWE

★

Mysterio was only
14 years old when he
debuted in Mexico.

Mysterio followed his uncle into lucha libre.
His first ring name was Colibrí. This is Spanish
for "hummingbird." The name fit his small size
and high-flying moves.

In time, Mysterio teamed up with his uncle.
He changed his name to Rey Mysterio, Jr.
Under this name, he started a famous feud
with a luchador called Psicosis.

A SHARED NAME

Mysterio's uncle wrestled
as Rey Misterio, Sr.

A WWE SUPERSTAR

WRESTLING NAME: Rey Mysterio

REAL NAME: Óscar Gutiérrez

BIRTHDATE: December 11, 1974

HOMETOWN: San Diego, California

HEIGHT: 5 feet, 6 inches (1.7 meters)

WEIGHT: 175 pounds (79 kilograms)

WWE DEBUT: 2002

FINISHING MOVE: 619

Mysterio came to WWE in 2002. He kept his mask but dropped "Jr." from his name. Fans immediately welcomed Mysterio as a face.

Mysterio has won many individual championships. He has also been on winning tag teams. Superstars Edge and Eddie Guerrero have partnered with him for title matches.

EDGE

EDDIE GUERRERO

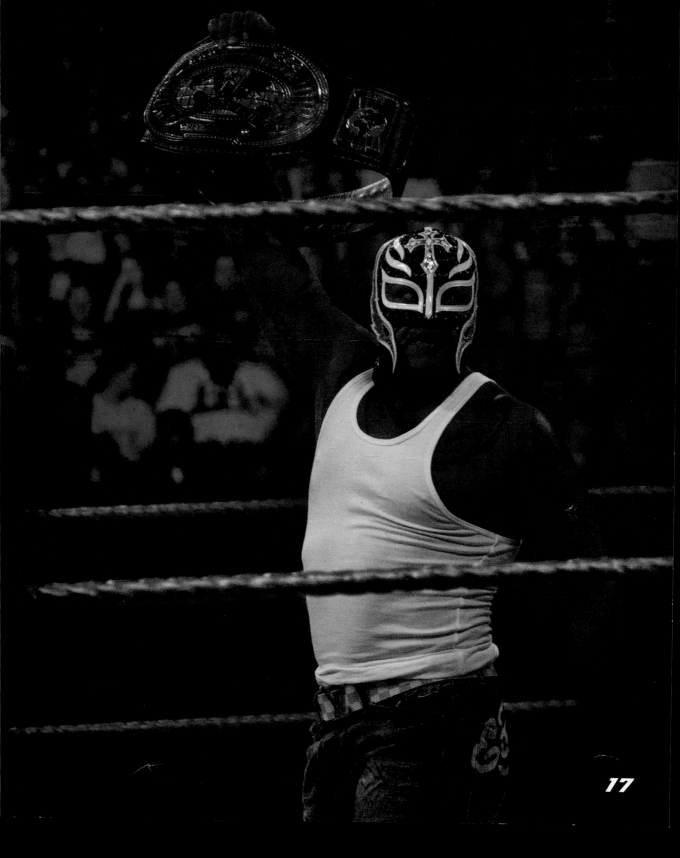

WINNING MOVES

Opponents get hit hard by Mysterio's 619. This finishing move is a powerful kick to the head. It begins with a swing between the ropes.

★

619 is the area code of
San Diego, California.
Mysterio named the move
after his hometown.

619

WEST COAST
POP

Mysterio jumps off the top rope for a West Coast Pop. He lands on his opponent's shoulders. Then he flips him onto the mat. This signature move grounds any challenger!

GLOSSARY

acrobatic moves—skills that require flexibility and involve jumping, twisting, and balancing

debut—first official appearance

face—a wrestler viewed as a hero

feud—a long-standing, heated rivalry between two people or teams

finishing move—a wrestling move that finishes off an opponent

fury—a violent, wild force

intimidated—frightened by a rival's power

lucha libre—professional wrestling in Mexico; lucha libre is known for high-flying moves.

luchadores—professional wrestlers in Mexico; luchadores wear masks and perform high-flying moves.

signature move—a move that a wrestler is famous for performing

tag teams—wrestling pairs that compete as teams

title matches—championship matches

TO LEARN MORE

At the Library

Black, Jake. *WWE General Manager's Handbook*. New York, N.Y.: Grosset & Dunlap, 2012.

Black, Jake. *WWE Supersized Activity Book*. New York, N.Y.: Grosset & Dunlap, 2012.

Markegard, Blake. *Alberto Del Rio*. Minneapolis, Minn.: Bellwether Media, 2015.

On the Web

Learning more about Rey Mysterio is as easy as 1, 2, 3.

1. Go to www.factsurfer.com.

2. Enter "Rey Mysterio" into the search box.

3. Click the "Surf" button and you will see a list of related web sites.

With factsurfer.com, finding more information is just a click away.

INDEX

The images in this book are reproduced through the courtesy of: Isabella Vosmikova/ Getty Images, front cover, p. 14; Devin Chen, front cover (small), pp. 8, 10; Matt Roberts/ Newscom, pp. 4, 18-19, 21; Z Sports Images/ Zuma Press/ Newscom, pp. 5, 11 (right), 20; David Seto, pp. 6, 12, 17; Shamsuddin Muhammad, p. 7; Michael Bezjian/ Getty Images, p. 9; Revelli-Beaumont/ SIPA/ Newscom, p. 11 (left); Rex USA/ Picture Perfect, p. 13; Jason L Nelson/ AdMedia/ Newscom, p. 16 (left); Graham Whitby/ Zuma Press, p. 16 (right).